LIFE SCIENCE

HUMAN BODY

Lauri Seidlitz

WEIGL PUBLISHERS INC.

Project Coordinator
Heather C. Hudak

Design
Bryan Pezzi

Cover Design
Terry Paulhus

Published by Weigl Publishers Inc.
350 5th Avenue, Suite 3304, PMB 6G
New York, NY 10118-0069

Website: www.weigl.com
Copyright ©2008 WEIGL PUBLISHERS INC.

All of the Internet URLs given in the book were valid at the time of
publication. However, due to the dynamic nature of the Internet, some
addresses may have changed, or sites may have ceased to exist since
publication. While the author and publisher regret any inconvenience
this may cause readers, no responsibility for any such changes can be
accepted by either the author or the publisher.

Library of Congress Cataloging-in-Publication Data

Seidlitz, Lauri.
  Human body / Lauri Seidlitz.
    p. cm. -- (Life science)
  Includes bibliographical references and index.
  ISBN 978-1-59036-705-6 (hard cover : alk. paper) -- ISBN 978-1-
59036-706-3 (soft cover : alk. paper)
  1. Body, human--Juvenile literature. 2. Human physiology--Juvenile
literature. I. Title.
  QP37.S45 2008
  612--dc22
                                    2007012621

Printed in the United States of America
1 2 3 4 5 6 7 8 9 0 11 10 09 08 07

Every reasonable effort has been made to trace ownership and to
obtain permission to reprint copyright material. The publishers would
be pleased to have any errors or omissions brought to their attention
so that they may be corrected in subsequent printings.

Contents

What Do You Know about the Human Body?

You may know more about the human body than you think. After all, you have a body of your own! Your body has many features in common with the people shown on this page. All of you have a head, a mouth, legs, and arms. Can you find eight other common features?

The human body has many features in common with other animals. Humans belong to a group of animals called mammals.

■ **Human beings look alike in many ways.**

4

Mammals all have hair or fur, warm blood, and young that drink their mothers' milk. Which mammal do you think is most like a human? Why?

Activity

Draw Mammals

Draw two mammals you might see in a zoo. How are they alike? How are they different?

How Other Mammals Are Like Humans			
Cheetahs	**Dogs**	**Gorillas**	**Whales**
Cheetah kittens drink milk from their mother.	Dogs have hair to protect their bodies.	Gorillas can change the expressions on their faces to communicate.	Whales breathe air to survive.

How Other Mammals Are Unlike Humans			
Cheetahs can run at speeds up to 70 miles (112 kilometers) an hour.	Dogs walk on four legs.	Gorillas use their long arms to help them walk.	Whales have **streamlined** bodies to help them swim in the ocean.

Every Body is Different

No two people in the world look exactly alike. Hair, skin, and eyes come in different colors. People's bodies are built differently. Their height, width, and weight are not the same. Even chins, lips, and noses have many sizes and shapes.

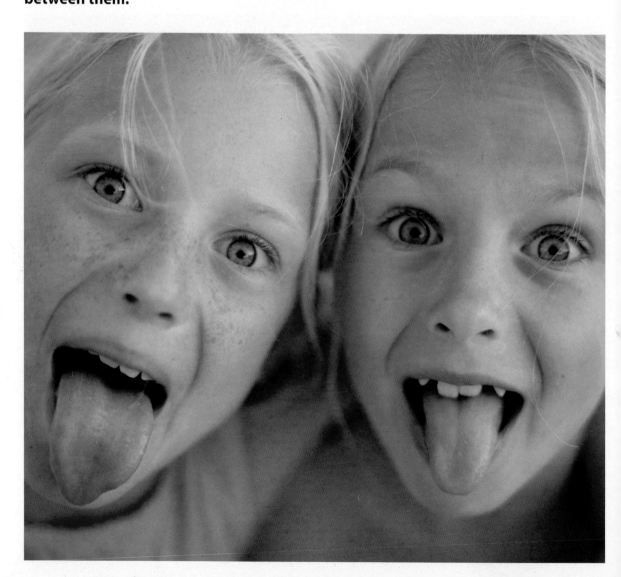

■ **People may look like their parents, grandparents, or other ancestors.**

We have many words that describe how people look. Eyes are blue, green, brown, or hazel. Hair is curly, straight, wavy, blond, brown, black, red, gray, thick, stringy, long, or short. Some people may not have hair. People are tall, short, or of average height. Human skin is smooth, wrinkled, black, red, brown, golden, freckled, pale, or tanned. Bodies are thin, muscular, plump, or somewhere in between. People from the same families can have similar features because they have the same **ancestors**.

■ **Body differences make each person one of a kind.**

Puzzler

Members of a family often look alike. If the mother has curly hair, and the father has straight hair, what kind of hair might the baby have?

Answer: This question has more than one right answer. The baby could have straight hair, curly hair, or something in between.

7

Fingerprint Detective

Every person in the world has a different skin pattern on his or her fingertips. This pattern exists even before we are born, and it never changes. We leave a copy of the pattern on everything we touch. The copy is called a fingerprint. Fingerprints come in three main patterns—arches, loops, and whorls.

■ Sometimes, fingerprints are easy to see if an object is dusted with powder.

FINGERPRINT PATTERNS		
Arches	Loops	Whorls

Police use fingerprints to find out who has committed a crime. They sprinkle a special powder on objects at the crime scene. This powder sticks to oily fingerprints and shows their pattern. Detectives compare these fingerprints to the fingerprints of people who might have committed the crime. They try to find a match.

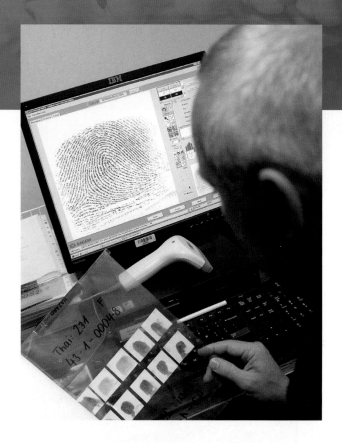

■ Scientists work in laboratories to prepare fingerprints for identification.

Activity

Solve the Crime

Detectives found two fingerprints at the scene of a crime. Can you find a match on this page?

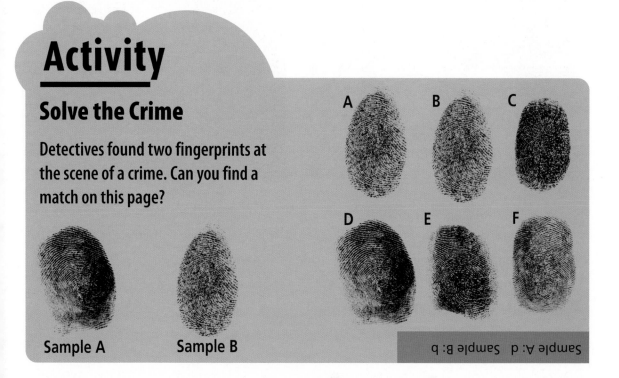

Sample A   Sample B

A   B   C

D   E   F

Sample A: d   Sample B: b

Body Structures

Structures inside and outside the human body protect it, help it move, and give it shape. Muscles and bones work together inside our bodies. They give our bodies support and strength. Skin, hair, and nails work as a protective outer surface.

Body Structures

Bones

- are strong, stiff parts that support the body
- form a frame for the body called a skeleton
- contain the red bone **marrow** that makes new blood cells

Hair and Nails

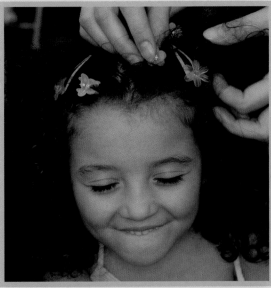

- are made of dead body cells
- help protect the body and keep it warm

Puzzler

Humans have seven bones in their necks. How many bones do you think a giraffe has in its neck?

Answer: A giraffe has the same number of neck bones as a human. The giraffe's bones are just much bigger!

Skin

- covers and protects the body
- helps control body temperature
- keeps fluids inside the body
- provides the sense of touch

Muscles

- can be **involuntary**, like the continually beating heart muscle
- can be **voluntary**, like the arm and leg muscles when you exercise
- pull bones to move different parts of the body

11

Body Systems

Groups of tissues that do special jobs in the body are called organs. Sometimes, many organs work together. They form a body organ system. Important body systems move **nutrients** around the body and help us breathe, digest food, and get rid of waste.

■ Our bodies try to take nutrients from everything we eat.

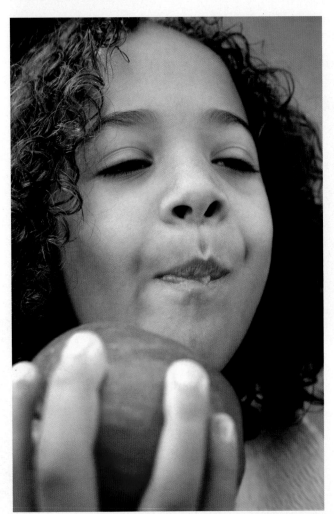

Digestion
People use teeth and jaws to chew food so that it is small enough to swallow. The stomach and **intestines** break the food into tiny nutrient pieces. Nutrients then go from the intestines to the blood.

Waste
The body cannot use everything that is eaten. Leftover waste ends up in the **bladder** or **rectum**. It then leaves the body.

■ The heart is a strong muscle that pumps blood through the body. It beats more than 100,000 times each day.

Circulation

Blood is a liquid. It moves through all parts of the body in a process called circulation. Blood carries nutrients and oxygen to all cells in the body. Cells need nutrients and oxygen to grow, do work, and repair themselves. Blood also carries away waste materials, such as **carbon dioxide**.

Breathing

We need oxygen to live. Lungs send oxygen from air we breathe in to the blood. Blood sends carbon dioxide, a body waste, to the lungs for the body to breathe out.

Activity

Get the Beat

Place two fingers lightly on the inside of your wrist below your thumb. Can you feel the beating? That is your heartbeat.

1. Count how many times your heart beats in one minute.

2. Record this number as your resting heart rate.

3. Run around or jump for one minute.

4. Count your heart rate again.

5. What change did you find? How do you think exercise affects the heart?

13

The Brain

The brain is the most important part of an organ system called the **nervous system**. Long, thin cells called nerves connect the brain to all parts of the body. Messages travel along neurons at speeds of 249 miles (400 kilometers) per hour.

■ Different parts of the brain control different senses and actions.

cerebrum

brain stem

cerebellum

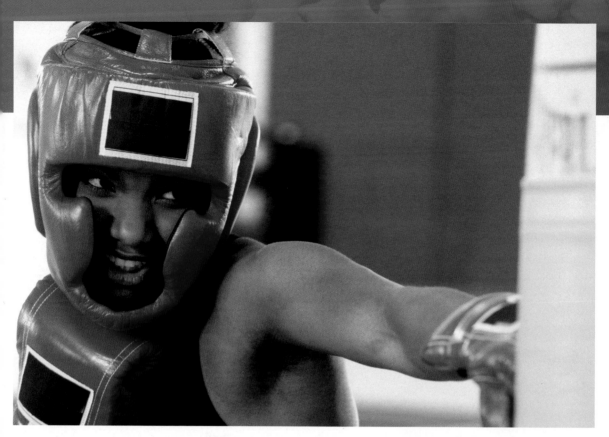

The brain is like a computer. It controls everything the body does. The brain tells our heart to speed up or slow down. It controls our breathing. The brain allows us to move, think, learn, and remember. It must be kept safe from harm.

■ Hard hats and helmets protect the head from injury. What jobs or sports require people to wear head protection?

Puzzler

The brain controls our breathing. It tells the body when to bring in more air. Take a deep breath, and hold it for as long as you can. Time yourself. What happens?

Answer: After about a minute, the brain knows the body needs more oxygen. It then forces you to breathe out used air and breathe in fresh air.

15

Senses

The tongue, ears, eyes, nose, and skin are sense organs. They send information about the world around us to the brain. The brain tells the body how to react. Do you know which sense belongs to each sense organ?

Sight
The eyes collect light and make a picture signal for the brain. The brain tells the body what it is seeing and how to respond.

Hearing
The outer ears collect sound and send it into the inner ears. The brain interprets the sound and tells us what we are hearing.

Puzzler

You can often tell which sense an animal uses most. Just look for its biggest sense organ. Which sense is most important to the animals in the photos? Which of your senses is most important to you?

a) Rabbit   **b) Lemur**   **c) Rhino**

Taste

Many tiny bumps called taste buds cover the tongue. Different parts of the tongue sense different tastes.

Touch

Tiny sensors in the skin let the brain know when the body is touching something. The brain tells the body how to react to everything the skin touches.

Smell

The nose detects smells in the air and signals the brain. The brain helps identify the smells.

Our Smallest Parts

All living things, including humans, are made of tiny living parts called cells. There are about 75 to 100 trillion cells in the human body. Cells are so small that 200 could fit onto the period at the end of this sentence. The body has many kinds of cells. Each kind does a different job in the body.

A microscope helps us look at cells and discover how they work.

Puzzler

All animals begin life as a single cell. The cell contains all the information needed to build a new animal, such as a dog, a bird, or a person. What instructions would a baby bird cell have that a baby human cell would not have?

Answer: Your answer might include instructions for building a beak, feathers, and wings.

A human begins to grow when cells from a mother and father combine. These two cells make a new cell that grows into a baby. This is the reason you may look like your mother or father. Your body was made from a tiny part of each of their bodies. Your parents were made from a tiny part of each of their parents.

■ Sometimes, brothers and sisters look alike. Often, they look very different. They may look like their mother, their father, or one of their parents' relatives.

Having a Baby

Human bodies grow very quickly before babies are born. They grow in their mothers' bodies during **pregnancy**. Food and oxygen from the mother's body help the baby grow. Nutrients from the mother's blood reach the baby through a tube called the umbilical cord.

Babies are born with all the parts they will ever have. These body parts grow larger and become more useful. The baby does not grow new parts after birth.

■ A human baby usually grows for nine months before it is ready to be born.

Babies depend on adults for food and protection until they learn how to take care of themselves. Many animals are born knowing how to take care of themselves. This knowledge is called instinct. Humans must learn almost everything from their parents and other adults.

■ Unlike humans, a baby moose can stand up within one hour of being born.

■ All mammals that give birth to live young have belly buttons. This is the spot where the umbilical cord was attached.

Puzzler

A mouse grows for 20 days before it is ready to be born. An African elephant grows 630 to 660 days. A deer grows around 200 days. Using this information, figure out how many days a cow needs to grow before it is born.

Answer: A deer is about the same size as a cow. A good guess would be close to the number of days for a deer. A cow actually grows about 284 days before it is ready to be born.

21

Childhood to Adolescence

Children grow and learn quickly. As they grow, they gain more control over their bodies. They are able to do more for themselves. Babies can drink milk and juice. Young children can eat solid foods, but their parents must feed them. Older children can feed themselves.

Humans learn by experience. They watch and listen to the world around them. They try new things. Babies must be watched carefully so they do not try something dangerous.

■ Children begin crawling when they are about nine months old. They start walking on their own when they are about fifteen months old.

Children keep growing until they are about 10 to 14 years old. After this time, children enter **adolescence**. Adolescence is the time when a child's body becomes more like an adult's. Humans usually finish growing by the time they are about 18 to 21 years old. After that, humans may gain weight, but they do not grow taller.

■ People grow two sets of teeth in their lifetime. As children grow, their baby teeth fall out to make room for permanent teeth.

■ As children reach adolescence, they become more and more independent.

Activity

Growth Chart

Make a growth chart for yourself. Ask your parents if you can make it on a wall or inside a closet door. Stand straight with your heels against the wall. Draw a short line with a pencil for your height. Label it with the date. Check your height, and mark it again every six months.

Adulthood

Adults do not grow, but their bodies continue to change. Body cells are always being created and repaired. Many animals, some humans included, spend their adulthood having children and raising them.

■ Gravity is the force that pulls objects towards Earth. Astronauts measure taller in space without the force of gravity on their bodies. When they return to Earth, they measure at normal height.

The body starts to wear out with age. The older a body becomes, the harder it is to fight off infections and disease. The body begins to wrinkle, and hair turns gray. Older people may even become shorter. The spaces between the bones in the **spine** shrink as people age.

The time an animal lives between its birth and death is called its life span. Many things affect how long an animal lives. Good food and healthy habits help people live longer.

■ The life expectancy for a human in the United States is 78 years. Exercise and healthy eating can help people live even longer.

Activity

Life Stages

Draw a picture of each of the following stages in the human life span.

- Adolescence
- Adulthood
- Infancy
- Childhood

Can you put the stages in the proper order?

■ The life span of a wild elephant is similar to a human's. These elephants can live up to 60 years.

Broccoli for Breakfast?

No single food can give your body everything it needs. Even a healthy food, such as broccoli, is not enough if that is all you eat. Your body needs many different nutrients. Nutritionists take special classes to learn which foods the body needs to stay healthy. Nutritionists say people should eat at least one serving from each level of the food group pyramid each day.

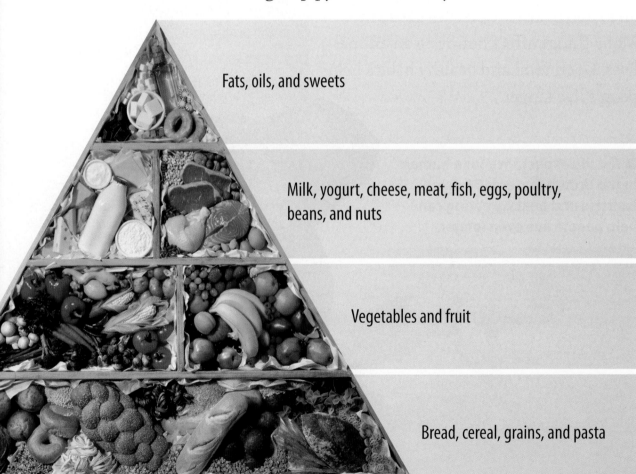

Fats, oils, and sweets

Milk, yogurt, cheese, meat, fish, eggs, poultry, beans, and nuts

Vegetables and fruit

Bread, cereal, grains, and pasta

Some nutritionists work in schools and teach children about healthy eating. Others plan meals for people who stay in hospitals. A nutritionist may even work with a sports coach to make sure athletes eat food that will give them more energy.

■ Nutritionists can help athletes perform at their best.

■ Nutritionists help people choose the best foods to eat to maintain a healthy weight.

Activity

Do Some Research

Many people have jobs working with the human body. Ask a parent or other adult to help you find out about the following careers.

- athlete
- biologist
- doctor
- fitness instructor
- nurse
- physiotherapist

Healthy Bodies

The human body does many jobs. It senses the world around itself. It makes decisions. It moves, works, plays, and talks. It needs to be healthy to do these jobs well. To stay healthy, a human body needs food, water, exercise, and rest.

Food provides nutrients, or fuel. Your body needs nutrients to do work. When you feel hungry, your body is saying your energy and nutrients are running low. When you feel sleepy, your body is saying it is time for rest.

■ Water is the best thing to drink when the body is thirsty.

■ After exercise, the body often requires rest to give muscles time to recover.

Here are a few ways to keep your body in shape.

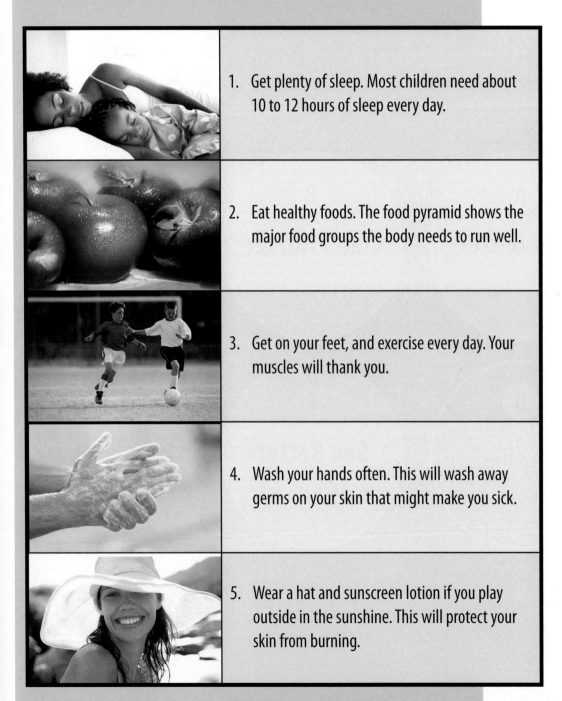

1. Get plenty of sleep. Most children need about 10 to 12 hours of sleep every day.

2. Eat healthy foods. The food pyramid shows the major food groups the body needs to run well.

3. Get on your feet, and exercise every day. Your muscles will thank you.

4. Wash your hands often. This will wash away germs on your skin that might make you sick.

5. Wear a hat and sunscreen lotion if you play outside in the sunshine. This will protect your skin from burning.

Beyond Our Bodies

We humans want to do many more things than our bodies let us do. People have made tools to help us see and hear farther, travel faster, and climb higher and lower. Which tool would you use to do the following?

A
Hear Better

B
Climb Higher

C
Move after Injury

D
Go Faster

E
See Better

F
Speak Louder

Answer: A) 1, B) 4, C) 2, D) 3, E) 6, F) 5

31

Glossary

adolescence: the stage when a child's body grows into adult form

ancestors: the people from whom you are descended, including your parents, grandparents, great-grandparents, and so on

bladder: a soft, thin bag in the body that holds liquid waste

carbon dioxide: a colorless, odorless gas that you exhale when you breathe

intestines: the long tubes of the stomach where the last stages of digestion take place

involuntary: done without thought or attention

marrow: soft, fatty tissue in the center of bones

nervous system: a system that connects the brain with the rest of the body

nutrients: substances in food the body needs in order to stay healthy

pregnancy: the condition in which a woman has a baby growing inside her

rectum: the end of the intestines, which collects waste from food

spine: the backbone needed for a person to sit and stand up

streamlined: shaped to allow air and water to move past easily

voluntary: moved by a person's own will

Index

Websites

www.bbc.co.uk/science/humanbody
www.medtropolis.com/VBody.asp

www.innerbody.com/htm/body.html
http://bam.gov

Some websites stay current longer than others. For further websites, use your search engines to locate topics such as circulation, fingerprints, nutrition, and teeth.